Dickmeyer   1982-83
Me

DATE DUE		
NOV 27 1983	SEP 3 0 2004	
MAY 28 1984	JUL 1 9 2007	
AUG. 6 1984	SEP 2 4 2019	
SEP. 28 1985		
NOV. 1 4 1985		
DEC. 7 1985		
OCT. 1 6 1986		
NOV. 0 5 1994		
MAY 2 3 2002		

FOOTBALL
is for me

FOOTBALL
is for me

Lowell A. Dickmeyer

photographs by
Alan Oddie

 Lerner Publications Company   Minneapolis

The author wishes to thank Jan Berard, Robert Brunette, the Al Hudson family, and the directors, coaches, parents, and players associated with the Newbury Park Athletic Association.

LIBRARY OF CONGRESS CATALOGING IN PUBLICATION DATA

Dickmeyer, Lowell A.
Football is for me.

(A Sports for Me Book)
SUMMARY: Eleven-year-old Mike explains how football is played, discusses equipment and training, and relates his first game as running back for his team.

1. Football—Juvenile literature. [1. Football] I. Oddie, Alan. II. Title. III. Series.

GV950.7.D52 1979   796.33′22   79-15445
ISBN 0-8225-1087-1

Manufactured in the United States of America. Published simultaneously in Canada by J. M. Dent & Sons (Canada) Ltd., Don Mills, Ontario.

International Standard Book Number: 0-8225-1087-1
Library of Congress Catalog Card Number: 79-15445

1 2 3 4 5 6 7 8 9 10 85 84 83 82 81 80 79

Hi! My name is Mike. I'm 11 years old, and I play football. My team is called the Bruins. I also like to watch professional football on television. My favorite pro team is the Dallas Cowboys.

My home is near the Cowboys' summer camp. Last summer, I watched the Cowboys work out every day, as soon as my chores were done. It was exciting to see the Cowboys at their practices. They made football look like fun, but I could tell that it was a lot of work, too.

After practices, I talked to some of the Cowboy players and asked them for their autographs. One day I finally met my favorite player, Tony Hill. I told him that I was going to play football, and that this would be my first year on a team. Tony was really nice. He showed me the right way to throw the football. And he said he would help me if I had any other questions.

That night after supper, I looked at some football books. As I read, I imagined myself in the pictures. I daydreamed about playing in the pros. Then people might ask for my autograph, too.

I knew I would have to practice hard for years and years to become a professional player. I could hardly wait for my first season to begin. But the Bruins' first practice was not until school started in the fall.

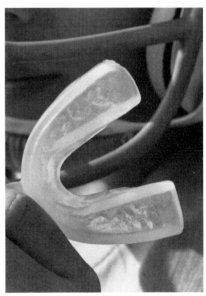

At our first practice, we got our football equipment. Football players need special equipment to keep from getting hurt. A helmet protects the head. The helmet has a face guard, a chin strap, and soft padding inside. Attached to the helmet is a plastic mouthpiece. Each player has his own special mouthpiece that fits around his teeth perfectly.

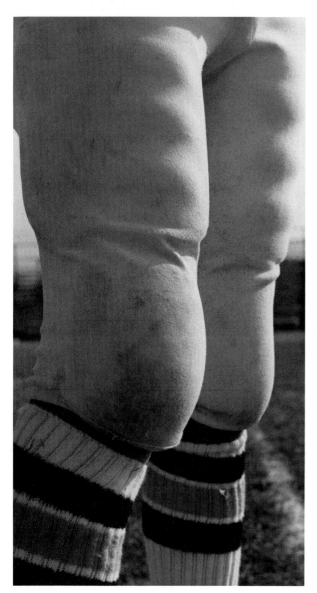

Football players also wear pads over their shoulders, hips, knees, and thighs. The pads are covered by the player's shirt, or jersey, and pants.

All of the Bruins wore leather shoes with rubber points, or **cleats.** The cleats give players a better grip on grass so that they can run faster.

We practiced on a regular football playing field. The playing field is 100 yards long and about half as wide. At each end is a **goal line.**

Between the goal lines are more lines spaced five yards apart. Behind the goal lines are the **end zones.** The **goal posts,** which are tall posts with a crossbar between them, stand at the back of the end zones.

Each football team has 22 players and many substitutes. A group of 11 players makes up the **offense**. The offense tries to score points for the team. The other 11 players are called the **defense**. The defense tries to prevent the opponents from scoring.

When the offense is on the field, the team has four plays, called **downs,** to try to move the ball forward at least 10 yards. The offense can move the ball by running with it or by throwing it. Throwing is also called **passing**.

If the offense succeeds in moving the ball 10 yards, the team is awarded another four downs to make another 10 yards. This continues until the offense scores or fails to make 10 yards. Then the opponents become the offense and try to move the ball.

The offense scores when it succeeds in moving the ball across the opponent's goal line. The offense scores a **touchdown** if the ball is run or passed into the end zone. A touchdown is worth six points. The team that scores a touchdown gets a chance to make a **conversion.** A one-point conversion, or **extra-point**, can be scored by kicking the ball over the crossbar on the goalpost. A two-point conversion can be scored by either running or passing the ball into the end zone from the three-yard line.

Sometimes the offense is close to the goal line, but the team does not think it will be able to score a touchdown. Then the team can use one of its downs to try to score a **field goal.** For a successful field goal, the ball must be kicked over the crossbar of the goalpost. A field goal is worth three points.

Before the Bruins actually began practicing football skills, we had several weeks of conditioning drills to get in shape. Coach Brunette said exercise would make us strong and fast. We would also be less likely to get injured.

We continued to exercise when our regular practices began. We did the bicycle exercise, belly rockers, leg lifters, and lots of stretching exercises. We also ran in place.

After practices, we ran wind sprints. All of us would line up at the end of the field. When Coach Brunette blew his whistle, we would run very fast for 20 yards. As soon as we were all lined up again, the whistle would blow. We barely had time to catch our breath before we had to run at top speed again.

Sometimes I got very tired and felt like quitting. Then I would stop by the Cowboy training camp and talk to Tony. He said that all football players get tired. But I should still always try my hardest. "Football is a team sport," Tony would say. "And everyone has to be in shape to do his job."

Each player on a football team has a very important job to do. At the start of each play, everyone lines up in a special position on the field. The players who crouch down in

the front line are called **linemen.** The players who stand behind the linemen make up the **backfield.**

The **center** is the offensive man who puts the ball in play. He stands over the ball and waits for a special signal from the quarterback. Then he snaps, or **hikes**, the ball between his legs to the quarterback's hands. The center's job is not over after the snap. Once the ball moves, the defense begins to move forward. It is the center's job to **block,** or stop, the defensive linemen.

21

The **quarterback** takes the ball from the center. It is the quarterback's job to run, pass, or hand off the ball to the running backs. The decision to run or pass the ball is usually made in the **huddle**. The offense meets in a huddle, or tight group, before a play begins.

A good football team mixes its running and passing plays. So the quarterback should be a good passer. On a pass play, the quarterback usually backpedals into the open space behind his blockers. Then he looks for a receiver. The ball is thrown with a snap of the wrist. The arm should continue to follow through.

Not everyone on offense can catch a pass. Only the **ends** and the running backs can be receivers. A good receiver tries to get into an open space on the field to catch the ball.

In our practices, we often combined passing and receiving drills. The coach reminded the receivers to keep their eyes on the ball until it was in their hands.

Pass receiving is only part of the job of the running backs. They are most often ball carriers on running plays. When you run with the ball, it is important to tuck the ball against your body. You have to run fast, but also be able to change directions quickly. Sometimes you have to "straight arm" the defensive man in order to side-step him.

A ball carrier cannot avoid all tackles. If you know you are about to be tackled, be sure to hold onto the ball. If your tackler jars the ball loose or you drop it, you have **fumbled.** This means the ball is free for either team to recover.

The two running backs who are not the ball carrier on a play become blockers for the runner. A blocker pushes defensive players away from the ball carrier. A good ball carrier follows his blockers because they can open up a clear path for running the ball.

The offensive linemen are also blockers. They are called **tackles** and **guards**. They line up in a **three-point stance**, ready to charge forward to block the defensive linemen.

To practice blocking, we used a **driving sled** like the one in this picture. We would take our stance low to the ground. On signal, we would explode out of our stance and push into the sled.

We would also practice using our bodies to block a defensive man. It is illegal for offensive linemen to use their arms to block, unless the arms are close to the body. If you use your hands, you can be given a penalty for **holding**.

Every good football team has a strong defense. The defense works together to stop the opponent's offense from scoring. The defense stops offensive players by tackling them, or bringing them to the ground. Remember to wrap your arms firmly around the player as you tackle him.

The defensive linemen are the four front men on defense. They are also called **tackles** and **ends.** They line up along the **line of scrimmage,** opposite the offensive linemen. The line of scrimmage is an imaginary line on either side of the ball at the start of every play. It is the defensive linemen's job to stop the ball carrier at or behind the line of scrimmage.

Three **linebackers** stand behind the defensive linemen. If a ball carrier gets past the linemen, the linebackers try to tackle him. On passing plays, the linebackers must drop back to guard, or cover, and tackle the pass receivers.

Two **cornerbacks** and two **safeties** make up the last line of defense. If a ball carrier gets past the linebackers, the cornerbacks and safeties must stop him to prevent a touchdown. It is also their job to cover pass receivers on long passing plays.

Sometimes the cornerbacks and safeties are in a **zone** defense. This means that each person is responsible for covering one section of the playing field. He must stop all passes in his special zone. Other times the defense plays **man-to-man.** This means that a defensive player has to cover only one player, wherever he goes on the field.

Kicking is another important part of any football game. Every game starts with a **kickoff.** The kicker takes a few running steps forward before kicking the ball, which is upright on a tee. There is also a kickoff at the start of the second half and after a score.

Another kind of kick is called a **punt.** If

the offense does not make at least 10 yards in four downs, the team has to give up the ball. Rather than turn the ball over on the spot, the offense can use its fourth down to kick the ball far down the field. Then the opponents will have to go many more yards to score a touchdown. For a punt, the center hikes the ball to the punter, who must catch it and kick it away.

A **place kick** is used to score a field goal and the extra point after a touchdown. The center hikes the ball back to a ball holder. The holder holds the ball upright while the kicker steps forward and boots the ball over the crossbar of the goalposts.

After several weeks of practice, it was time for the Bruins' first real game. That same Saturday, the Dallas Cowboys were going to play an exhibition game. My parents were going to take me to the Cowboys game after my game was over.

My stomach was full of butterflies before my game. I was going to play running back

on offense. Coach Brunette called the Bruins together on the sidelines for a pep talk. He told us to play hard but clean. Just before we ran on to the field, he yelled, "What's your favorite game?"

We yelled back, "Football!"

The game was really exciting. It was half-time before we knew it. As we rested, Coach

Brunette said that we had too many pen-alties in the first half. For each penalty, the referee took away some of our yards because we broke some rules. Jim was called for holding. And Matt was penalized for grab-bing an opponent's face mask. Our team was also **offside**. This means that some of our players moved forward before the ball was snapped.

We played the second half determined not to break any rules. Our offense began to move the ball better, but we just couldn't score. Luckily our defense played well. Three times they tackled the quarterback behind the line of scrimmage. This is called **sacking** the quarterback.

The defense held our opponents to one touchdown. We kept trying to score, too. Just when things looked bad, Brian made a great **interception**. An interception happens when a defensive player steals a ball intended for an offensive player. The Bruins were really charged up. On the very next play, we scored! The game ended in a tie.

It was an exciting finish to a good game. Now I had the Cowboys game to look forward to. My parents bought me a Cowboys pennant. The stands were full, and we cheered whenever someone made a good play. I cheered extra loud when Tony scored a touchdown.

I couldn't wait to see Tony the next week after practice. He smiled when he saw me and gave me a big hug. We talked about our games as we walked to the Cowboys locker room. We both agreed that football was for us!

Words about FOOTBALL

BACKFIELD: The offensive and defensive players who play behind the linemen

BLOCK: The method used by an offensive player to push away an opponent. The blocker can use only his body or arms, as long as the arms are close to the body.

CLIP: An illegal block done on a defensive player from behind

DEFENSE: The team **not** in possession of the ball; the players who try to stop the other team from scoring

DOWN: An offensive play. A team is given four downs to try to gain at least 10 yards.

FIELD GOAL: To place kick the ball between the goal posts. A field goal is worth three points.

FIRST DOWN: The first of four downs awarded to an offense that has just gained possession of the ball or has just gained at least 10 yards

FUMBLE: To drop the football, making it a free ball for either team to recover

GOAL LINES: The final lines between the playing field and the end zones at the zero yard lines

HASH MARKS: Lines on the playing field parallel to the sidelines. All offensive plays start between or on the hash marks. When the ball goes outside these marks, an official brings it back to the closest hash mark to start the next play.

HUDDLE: A tight group of offensive players who gather behind the line of scrimmage to discuss the next play of the game

INTERCEPTION: A catch by a defensive player of a pass intended for an offensive player

KICKOFF: The method of starting play at the beginning of the game, at the start of the second half, after a touch down, and after a field goal

LINE OF SCRIMMAGE: The imaginary line to the right and left of the football, extending across the width of the field. The line of scrimmage separates the offense and the defense before play begins.

LINEMEN: Offensive and defensive players who begin play at the line of scrimmage

OFFENSE: The team in possession of the ball; the scoring unit of a team

OFFSIDE: A penalty called when an offensive or defensive player crosses the line of scrimmage before the ball is snapped

PENALTY: The yardage lost by a team for breaking a rule

PUNT: A kick on fourth down that sends the ball deep into the opponent's territory

TACKLE: The method used by a defensive player to bring a ball carrier to the ground

TOUCHDOWN: Six points awarded to a team for passing or running the ball into the opponent's end zone

The Playing Field

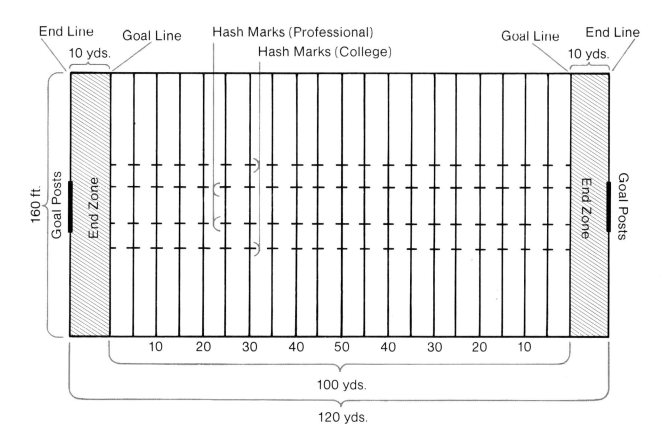

ABOUT THE AUTHOR

LOWELL A. DICKMEYER is active in athletics as a participant, instructor, and writer. He is particularly interested in youth sport programs, and each summer he organizes sports camps for hundreds of youngsters. Mr. Dickmeyer has been a college physical education instructor and an elementary school principal in southern California.

ABOUT THE PHOTOGRAPHER

ALAN ODDIE was born and raised in Scotland. He now resides in Santa Monica, California. In addition to his work as a photographer, Mr. Oddie is an author and a producer of educational filmstrips. He is currently the staff photographer for *Franciscan Communications*.